DATE DUE

MAR 0 7

GAYLORD

PRINTED IN U.S.A.

Grasshopper

Elizabeth J. Scholl

KIDHAVEN PRESS

An imprint of Thomson Gale, a part of The Thomson Corporation

Detroit • London • Munich

LIBRARY OF CONGRESS CATALOGING-IN-PUBLICATION DATA

Scholl, Elizabeth J.
   Grasshopper / by Elizabeth J. Scholl.
     p. cm.—(Bugs)
Includes bibliographical references and index.
Summary: Describes the physical characteristics of grasshoppers, their life cycle, where they live, and their eating habits.
   ISBN 0-7377-1771-8 (hardback : alk. paper)
   1. Grasshopper—Juvenile literature. [1. Grasshopper.] I. Title. II. Series.

Printed in China

CONTENTS

Chapter 1
Champion Jumpers   5

Chapter 2
A Grasshopper's Life   12

Chapter 3
Finding the Perfect Home   18

Chapter 4
Enormous Appetites   24

Glossary   29
For Further Exploration   30
Index   31
Picture Credits   32

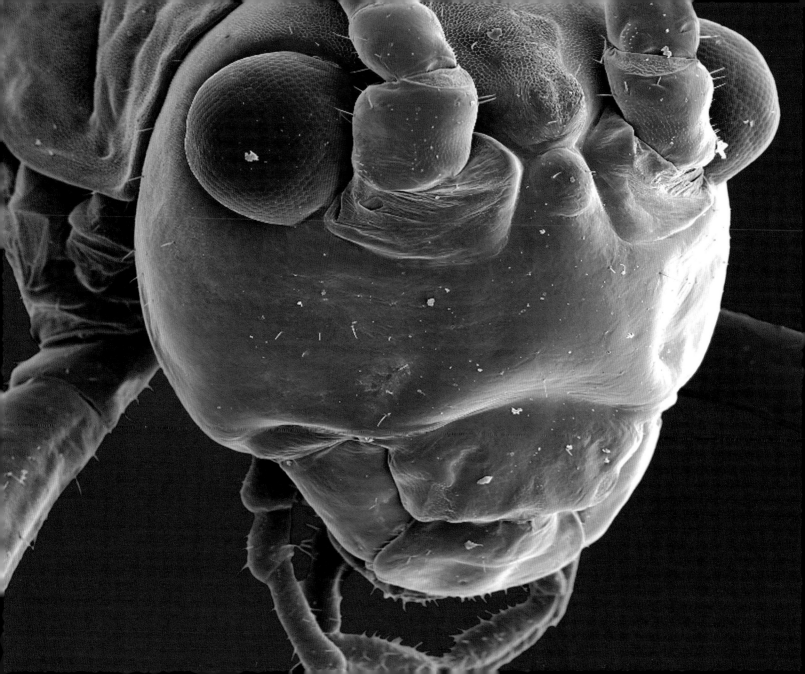

Champion Jumpers

Grasshoppers are found in all parts of the world except the Arctic. **Entomologists** have identified eighteen thousand species of grasshoppers. They are part of the insect order Orthoptera.

Most grasshoppers range between one and five inches in length. Some are smaller. The South African *Lithidium pusillium* grows to less than half an inch.

Opposite: A grasshopper head has been magnified many times its normal size.

Others can reach ten inches in length. The *Tropidacris cristatus* of Costa Rica is so large that one scientist mistook one for a bird and shot it while hunting bird specimens.

Long Jumpers

Grasshoppers are well known for their ability to jump. Some can leap up to twenty times their body's length. The world's largest grasshopper, the ten-inch-long *Tropidacris latrellei*, can jump fifteen feet. That is like a person jumping nearly one hundred feet!

Types of Grasshoppers

There are three types of grasshoppers. Many of the most common grasshoppers are in the short-horned grasshopper family. This family includes locusts. Locusts and other short-horned grasshoppers have antennae shorter than their bodies. They have hearing organs called **tympana**, located on the sides of their abdomens. Short-horned grasshoppers live in many different habitats including meadows and marshes.

Long-horned grasshoppers like the meadow grasshopper (below) have very long antennae, while short-horned grasshoppers like the locust (right) have very short antennae.

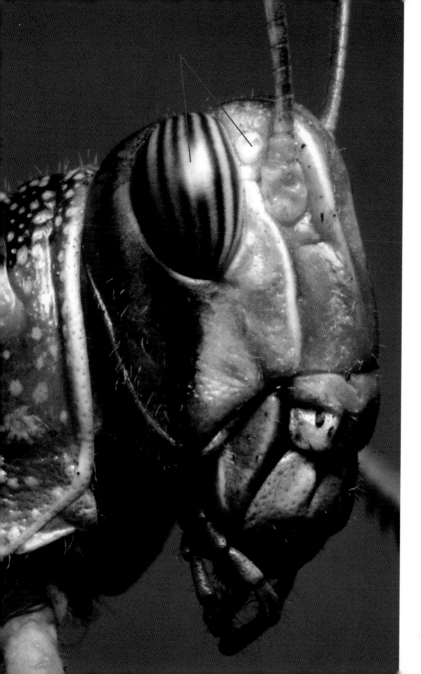

The long-horned grasshopper family includes katydids and meadow grasshoppers. This family of grasshoppers is found mostly in trees, bushes, and shrubs. Long-horned grasshoppers have antennae longer than the length of their bodies. They are usually green. Their tympana are located near the knee joints of their front legs.

The third type of grasshopper is known as the pygmy grasshopper. This family of grasshoppers includes the leaf-rolling grasshopper, found in the southern United States. Pygmy grasshoppers are the smallest of the grasshoppers. They grow to less than three-quarters of an inch in length. Pygmy grasshoppers have a shield that extends the length of the abdomen. It protects both the abdomen and the thorax.

Body Parts

Like all insects, the grasshopper's main body parts are the head, thorax, and abdomen. Two antennae on the head help the grasshopper sense food. The antennae allow the grasshopper to smell and touch.

Grasshoppers have five eyes. Two are compound eyes. Each compound eye has thousands of single lenses. These enable the grasshopper to see in front of it, behind it, and to each side. Its three single eyes, one above, one below, and one in between the antennae, help the grasshopper to see light and dark.

Most grasshoppers have two pairs of wings attached to the thorax. The leathery front wings protect the more delicate back wings. Some species, such as the meadow grasshopper, have short wings and are unable to fly. Others, like the plains lubber, have no wings at all. Generally, grasshoppers fly for just a few seconds at a time. Their wings help them jump farther or change direction. A few types of grasshoppers, such as locusts, fly long distances.

Opposite: With their large compound eyes and smaller single eyes, grasshoppers can sense light and dark, as well as see in all directions.

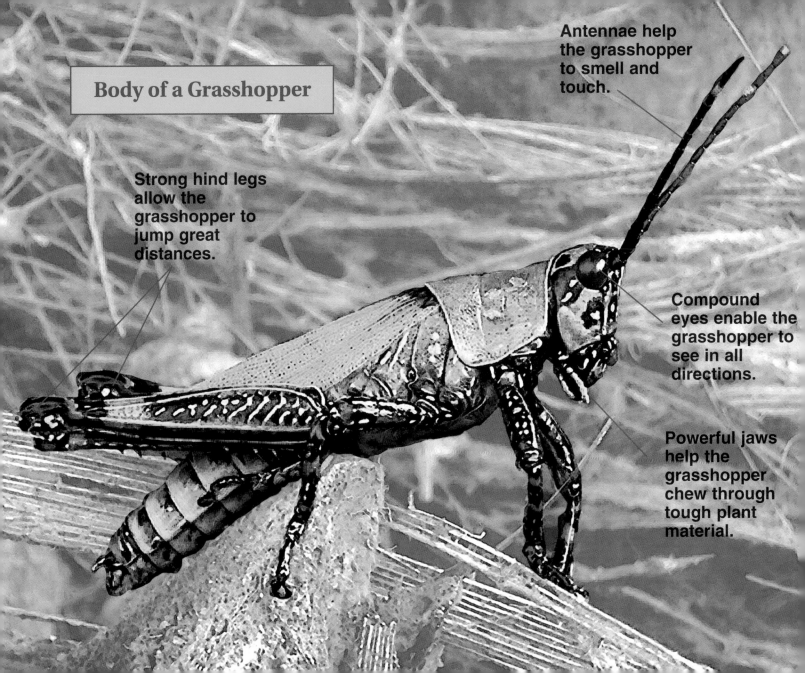

Body of a Grasshopper

Antennae help the grasshopper to smell and touch.

Strong hind legs allow the grasshopper to jump great distances.

Compound eyes enable the grasshopper to see in all directions.

Powerful jaws help the grasshopper chew through tough plant material.

The desert locust, for example, can travel eighty miles (and sometimes more) in a day.

The grasshopper's legs are also attached to the thorax, with four in front and two in back. The front legs hold food, and the strong hind legs help it jump. Grasshoppers use all six legs to walk.

The Abdomen

The grasshopper digests food in its abdomen. The abdomen also contains the parts of the grasshopper used for **reproduction**. The female stores eggs in her abdomen and uses the end of her abdomen to dig a hole for her eggs.

Grasshoppers are insects with many unique features. Special characteristics, such as powerful hind legs for jumping and strong jaws for chewing leaves, have helped grasshoppers survive in diverse habitats around the world.

A Grasshopper's Life

Opposite: During the mating process, the male grasshopper (right) sings to attract a female (left).

A grasshopper goes through three stages of life. It begins as an egg, hatches into a nymph, and finally reaches adulthood. In warm climates a grasshopper may live for several years, but in colder climates a grasshopper hatches in the spring and dies when the weather turns cold.

Mating

The life cycle of the grasshopper begins when male and female grasshoppers mate. A male grasshopper sings to
attract a female. The singing is called
stridulation. Some grasshoppers rub
their wings together to stridulate. Others rub their leg against their wing to
make this sound.

Some females respond by stridu-
lating back softly, letting the male
know she is ready to mate, but others
are silent. Each species has its own
song. A female grasshopper recognizes
the song made by the male of her
species.

Some types, such as the rufous
grasshopper, also perform to attract
mates. Males move their heads, stridulate, and turn their antennae around
like windmills to attract females. Male
band-winged grasshoppers attract

females by flying and showing off their brightly colored wings, which they sometimes snap together.

When grasshoppers mate, the male usually perches on the back of the female. He curls the tip of his abdomen beneath hers and inserts a capsule called a **spermatophore** into the female. Mating may last several hours. After mating, the female lays her eggs.

Eggs

The female grasshopper has an abdomen that stretches out like a telescope. At the end of her abdomen is an **ovipositor**, or egg depositer. The ovipositor is like a sword. It is used to help the grasshopper make hiding places for her eggs. The ovipositor can dig holes in the ground as well as slit leaf and plant stems.

A female lays anywhere from just a few to about 120 eggs at a time. Long-horned grasshoppers lay their eggs in low bushes or in cracks in tree trunks. Short-horned grasshoppers usually lay their eggs in

Opposite: Grasshopper nymphs (inset) hatch from eggs (pictured) in the spring.

holes in the ground. Pygmy grasshoppers often lay single eggs in small grooves in the soil.

After depositing her eggs, the grasshopper sprays a sticky substance over the eggs. This soon hardens into a protective waterproof case, called an **ootheca**. A female grasshopper usually makes several oothecae.

In colder climates, oothecae can survive the snow, freezing temperatures, and winds of winter. Nymphs hatch in the spring. In warm climates, eggs may hatch in three weeks.

From Nymph to Adult

Nymphs, or young grasshoppers, look much like adults. But they are smaller, often lighter in color, and their wings are not fully developed.

As grasshoppers grow, they shed their skin (above left) several times.

Grasshopper nymphs typically **molt** four or five times before they become adults. This is called metamorphosis. During molting the nymph sheds its skin, or **exoskeleton**. The old skin splits down the back because the nymph has outgrown it. A larger skin has formed under the old one. It takes six to eight weeks for a nymph to grow into an adult.

When grasshoppers have grown into adults, they are ready to look for mates. The adult grasshoppers will begin another life cycle.

Grasshoppers mature into fully grown adults in six to eight weeks.

Finding the Perfect Home

Opposite: Grasshoppers live in a variety of habitats, including forests, gardens, and meadows.

Grasshoppers do not build homes. They find them. Whether they live in forests, meadows, near ponds, or in gardens, they find homes among plants. Usually they live on the plants that provide them with food. When they eat themselves out of house and home, they move on.

Grasshopper Lifestyles

Generalist plant eaters, species that eat many kinds of plants, such as the American bird grasshopper, move from place to place. They make their homes on one species of plant until they get their fill and then move to another species. Others, such as the rainbow grasshopper, move frequently, nibbling from a variety of plants.

Certain grasshoppers live on the same type of plant all the time. The creosote bush grasshopper eats only one type of plant, spending most of its life on a single creosote bush.

Unusual Homes

Some grasshoppers make their homes in unusual places. The *Marellia remipes* of South America lives on aquatic plants such as the water poppy. The large marsh grasshopper is found on the plants that thrive in bogs and marshes of England and Ireland. The desert locust lives in the dry scrub brush of the deserts of North Africa, the Middle East, and Asia.

Opposite: Grasshoppers usually live on the same plants that provide them with food.

Grasshoppers often find homes near open areas where they can bask in the sun. When temperatures drop to sixty degrees Fahrenheit or lower at night, grasshoppers become unable to move. As temperatures warm up in the morning, sitting in the sun raises their body temperature, and they are able to move around again. Large-headed grasshoppers of the grasslands of the United States bask for several hours early in the day, becoming active in midmorning. They spend most of the day among the tall grasses and then bask again in the late afternoon. Their nighttime homes are on the lower part of grass stems or on the ground.

Blending In

Many grasshoppers, such as the gray bird grasshopper and the green bird grasshopper found in the Sonoran Desert of Arizona, make their homes on plants the same color as they are. By blending in with the color of the soil or with the plants it lives on, a grasshopper has a better chance of survival.

Ground-dwelling varieties such as the reddish pallid-winged grasshoppers blend in perfectly with the red soil they live on. Other species that live on dark soil are brown and black, and those that live on white soil are white. Slant-faced grasshoppers have bands along their body that mimic the grass stalks they often cling to. Creosote bush grasshoppers are olive green with shiny patches, just like the leaves of the creosote bush on which they live.

Grasshoppers all over the world are experts in finding places to live that provide them with both food and protection from predators. Blending in with their surroundings and eating a variety of plants enable them to thrive wherever they make their homes.

Opposite: Many grasshoppers, like this slant-faced grasshopper, live on plants the same color as they are in order to hide from predators.

CHAPTER

4

Enormous Appetites

Grasshoppers are mainly vegetarians, feeding on leaves and flowers. They chew with two sets of powerful jaws, called mandibles. With their jaws and sharp teeth, they slice and grind up their meals.

Grasshoppers eat many of the same plants people eat, including wheat, barley, corn, rye, and oats. Some eat fruits and vegetables. A few grasshoppers, such as the plains lubber, eat insects, including other grasshoppers. Other species of grasshoppers eat dung.

Most grasshoppers are **solitary** creatures. They live most of their lives alone. As solitary insects, grasshoppers do not cause much damage to farm crops.

However, certain types of short-horned grasshoppers can cause tremendous destruction. Locusts are one type. Locusts sometimes gather in large groups called **swarms**. Locust swarms have been known to contain as many as 124 billion insects.

A locust swarm looks like a massive cloud. The swarm flies along, following the direction of the wind, sometimes traveling sixty to seventy miles a day. When the swarm spots green vegetation, such as a wheat field, it swoops down, flies through, and quickly eats the entire crop. Each locust eats its own body weight in food each day, about half an ounce. Large locust swarms have been known to consume up to three hundred thousand tons of food in one day.

The largest recorded locust swarm occurred in the midwestern United States in 1875. The swarm of

Grasshoppers use their powerful jaws to chew plants and flowers.

A swarm of locusts looks like a huge cloud and can eat thousands of tons of food in a single day.

Rocky Mountain locusts was 1,800 miles long and 110 miles wide. It was the size of Connecticut, Delaware, New York, New Jersey, Maryland, Massachusetts, Pennsylvania, Rhode Island, Vermont, and New Hampshire combined. The swarm destroyed buckwheat, barley, tobacco, wheat, corn, and vegetables. It even ate through laundry hung out to dry on clotheslines, as well as fence posts, dead animals, and wool, which the locusts ate right off the sheep.

Escaping Predators

The natural enemies of grasshoppers are numerous. They include flies, beetles, spiders, birds, frogs, snakes, and rodents. Grasshoppers have a number of ways to protect themselves from being eaten.

The band-winged grasshopper escapes predators by leaping suddenly and spreading its wings to reveal bold colored patterns. The predator will look for the bright colors, but the grasshopper will be hiding on the ground several feet away, having folded its wings back under and becoming drab brown again.

An Eastern screech owl gobbles down a grasshopper.

Toxic Grasshoppers

Some grasshoppers use their bright colors to advertise that they are poisonous. The rainbow grasshopper is black with bright blue, red, yellow, and white markings. They get toxins, or poisons, from certain plants they eat, and the colors let the potential predators know they are not safe to eat.

Grasshoppers have other ways of discouraging predators. Some throw up, or regurgitate their food to create an unpleasant odor. Others have the ability to release a leg. So, if a predator grabs the grasshopper's leg, the grasshopper can escape by leaving its leg behind. (It will not grow a new one.)

Grasshoppers are some of the world's most adaptable insects. Though they have many enemies, their techniques of protecting themselves from predators, as well as their skill at finding food sources, have enabled them to survive for millions of years.

Grasshoppers are some of the world's most successful insects.

GLOSSARY

entomologist: A scientist who studies insects.

exoskeleton: An external, protective covering of an animal.

molt: To shed outer skin, with cast-off parts being replaced by new growth.

ootheca: A protective case for an insect's eggs.

ovipositor: A specialized organ for depositing eggs.

reproduction: The act of producing offspring, or young.

solitary: Living alone.

spermatophore: A capsule or pocket enclosing sperm.

stridulation: Producing a noise by rubbing together special body parts.

swarm: A large group moving together.

tympana: The hearing organs of a grasshopper or other insect.

FOR FURTHER EXPLORATION

Books

Amanda Harman, *Nature's Children: Grasshoppers*. Danbury, CT: Grolier, 2001. This book discusses the types of grasshoppers found around the world. It describes their body parts, habits, and life cycles.

Janet Hoffman, *Grasshoppers*. Mankato, MN: Smart Apple Media, 1999. This short but informative book has lovely photographs and chapters describing grasshopper habitats, body parts, life cycles, songs, and enemies.

Sylvia A. Johnson, *Chirping Insects*. Minneapolis: Lerner, 1986. This book offers a description of all types of grasshoppers and other members of the Orthoptera order of insects. The close-up photographs and in-depth explanations are interesting and informative.

Sarah Swan Miller, *Grasshoppers and Crickets of North America*. Danbury, CT: Franklin Watts, 2003. Descriptive text and vivid photographs offer an interesting picture of grasshoppers and their close relatives, crickets.

Web Sites

How Grasshoppers Jump (www.st-andrews. ac.uk/~wjh/jumping/forcespd.htm). This is the Web site of William Heitler, professor of biology at the University of St. Andrews in Scotland. This Web site has a fascinating, though scientific, explanation of how grasshoppers jump.

National Wildlife Federation (www. enature.com). Visitors to this site can type the word *grasshopper* into the search box and find descriptions and photos of twenty-two species of grasshoppers.

INDEX

abdomen, 11
American bird grasshoppers, 20
antennae, 8, 9
appearance, 6, 8
aquatic plants, 20

band-winged grasshoppers, 13–14, 27–28
blending, 23
body, 8–9, 17
body temperatures, 21

compound eyes, 9
creosote bush grasshoppers, 20, 23

desert locusts, 11, 20
dung, 25

eggs, 11, 14, 16
exoskeleton, 17
eyes, 9

flying, 9, 11, 13–14
food, 20, 24, 25

gray bird grasshoppers, 23
green bird grasshoppers, 23

hearing, sense of, 6
homes, 19–23

jaws, 24

jumping, 6

katydids, 8

large-headed grasshoppers, 21
leaf-rolling grasshoppers, 8
legs, 11, 13, 28–29
life cycle, 12
life span, 12
Lithidium pusillium, 5
locust(s)
  family, 6
  flying, 9, 11
  homes, 20
  swarms, 25, 27
long-horned grasshoppers, 8, 14

mandibles, 24
Marellia remipes, 20
marsh grasshoppers, 20
mating, 13–14
meadow grasshoppers, 8, 9
metamorphosis, 17
molting, 16–17

nymphs, 16–17

ootheca, 16
ovipositor, 14

pallid-winged grasshoppers, 23

plains lubber grasshoppers, 9, 25
poisons, 28
predators, escaping, 27–29
pygmy grasshoppers, 8, 16

rainbow grasshoppers, 20, 28
range, 5
reproduction, 11, 13–14, 16–17
rufous grasshoppers, 13

short-horned grasshoppers, 6, 14
sight, sense of, 9
single eyes, 9
size, 5, 6, 8
slant-faced grasshoppers, 23
spermatophere, 14
stridulation, 13
sun basking, 21
swarms, 25, 27

temperatures, 21
thorax, 9, 11
toxins, 28
Tropidacris cristatus, 6
Tropidacris latrellei, 6
tympana, 6, 8
types, 5, 6

vision, 9

wings, 9, 13–14

PICTURE CREDITS